PIANO • VOCAL • GUITAR

THE GREAT LYRICISTS

of Broadway, Hollywood & Tin Pan Alley

ISBN 0-7935-5986-3

HAL•LEONARD®
CORPORATION
7777 W. BLUEMOUND RD. P.O. BOX 13819 MILWAUKEE, WI 53213

Visit Hal Leonard Online at
www.halleonard.com

CONTENTS

THE GREAT LYRICISTS OF BROADWAY, HOLLYWOOD & TIN PAN ALLEY

Highlights of the careers of the lyricists featured in this folio are listed below. An * indicates that the lyricist(s) is also the bookwriter or screenwriter. In the individual song listings, a + indicates that the song won an Academy Award. The composer's name is listed in parenthesis after the show, film or song name.

HOWARD ASHMAN
(1950–1991)

Music by Alan Menken unless otherwise indicated.

Written for the stage:
1982 *Little Shop of Horrors**
1986 *Smile* (Marvin Hamlisch)
1994 *Beauty and the Beast* - adaptation of screen musical
        (additional lyrics by Tim Rice)

Written for the screen :
1986 *Little Shop of Horrors** (Geffen/Warner Brothers)
1989 *The Little Mermaid* (Ashman also co-producer - Disney)
1991 *Beauty and the Beast* (Disney)
1992 *Aladdin* (additional songs by Menken and Tim Rice - Disney)

A selection of individual songs:
Beauty and the Beast + (1991)
Be Our Guest (featured in this folio - 1991)
Friend Like Me (1992)
Kiss the Girl (1989)
Little Shop of Horrors (1983)
Part of Your World (1989)
Under the Sea+ (1989)

IRVING BERLIN (Israel Baline)
(1888-1989)

Berlin's amazing career began in 1909 with interpolations into Broadway scores. His first complete Broadway score was written in 1914. He wrote the music to most of his immense catalog of songs.

Written for the stage:
1911, 1916, 1918, 1919, 1920, 1927
        Ziegfeld Follies
1921-1924
        Music Box Revue (Berlin was co-owner of the Music Box Theatre)
1925 *The Cocoanuts*
1932 *Face the Music*
1933 *As Thousands Cheer*
1940 *Louisiana Purchase*
1946 *Annie Get Your Gun*
1949 *Miss Liberty*
1950 *Call Me Madam*
1962 *Mr. President*

Written for the screen:
1929 *The Cocoanuts* (Paramount)
1935 *Top Hat* (RKO)
1936 *Follow the Fleet* (RKO)
        On the Avenue (20th Century-Fox)
1938 *Alexander's Ragtime Band* (20th Century-Fox)
        Carefree (RKO)
1942 *Holiday Inn* (Paramount)
1946 *Blue Skies* (Paramount)
1948 *Easter Parade* (MGM)
1950 *Annie Get Your Gun* (MGM)
1953 *Call Me Madam* (20th Century-Fox)
1954 *There's No Business Like Show Business* (20th Century-Fox)
        White Christmas (Paramount)

Berlin, continued

A selection of individual songs:
Alexander's Ragtime Band (1911)
All Alone (1924)
Always (1925)
Blue Skies (1927)
Cheek to Cheek (1935)
Easter Parade (1933)
God Bless America (1938)
How Deep Is the Ocean (1932)
I Got the Sun in the Morning (1946)
I've Got My Love to Keep Me Warm (1937)
Let's Face the Music and Dance (1936)
Marie (1928)
A Pretty Girl Is Like a Melody (1919)
Puttin' On the Ritz (featured in this folio - 1929)
Say It Isn't So (1932)
Steppin' Out with My Baby (1948)
There's No Business Like Show Business (1946)
Top Hat, White Tie and Tails (1935)
What'll I Do? (1924)
White Christmas+ (1942)

LEW BROWN and B.G. "BUDDY" DeSYLVA
(Louis Brownstein and George Gard)
(1893-1958 and 1895-1950)

Music by Ray Henderson unless otherwise indicated.

Written for the stage:
1919 *La-La-Lucille!* (DeSylva with Arthur Jackson; music
        by George Gershwin)
1920 *Sally* (De Sylva with Clifford Grey; music by Jerome Kern)
1924 *Sweet Little Devil* (DeSylva; music by George Gershwin)
1925 *Tell Me More!* (DeSylva; music by George Gershwin)
1925, 1926, 1928, 1931
        George White's Scandals
        (Note: DeSylva had been a lyricist for the 1922-1924 editions
        of the Scandals)
1927 *Good News!* (Book by DeSylva and Lawrence Schwab)
1929 *Follow Thru*
1930 *Flying High*
1931 *George White's Scandals* (some sketches by Brown and Harry Conn;
        lyrics by Brown, music by Henderson)
1933 *Strike Me Pink* (sketches by Brown and Henderson, Jack McGowan and
        Mack Gordon; lyrics by Brown, music by Henderson)
1939 *DuBarry Was a Lady* (Book by DeSylva and Herbert Fields, music and
        lyrics by Cole Porter; DeSylva also produced)

Written for the screen:
1928 *The Singing Fool* (Warner Brothers)
1929 *Sunny Side Up* (Fox)
1930 *Follow Thru* (Paramount)
        Hold Everything (Warner Brothers)
        Just Imagine (Fox)
1931 *Flying High* (MGM)

Brown and DeSylva, continued

Lew Brown was the lyricist for the following musicals; composers and studios are listed in parenthesis.

1934 *Stand Up and Cheer* (Jay Gorney - Fox) [screenplay by Brown and Ralph Spence]
1936 *The Music Goes Round* (Harry Akst - Columbia)
       Strike Me Pink (Harold Arlen Goldwyn/UA)
1943 *I Dood It* (co-lyricist with Ralph Freed; Sammy Fain - MGM)
       Swing Fever (co-lyricist with Ralph Freed; Sammy Fain - MGM)

Note: B.G. DeSylva was a motion picture producer in Hollywood from 1938-1945.

A selection of individual DeSylva, Brown and Henderson songs:
The Best Things in Life Are Free (1927)
The Birth of the Blues (1926)
Black Bottom (1926)
Button Up Your Overcoat (featured in this folio - 1929)
I'm A Dreamer, Aren't We All (1929)
If I Had a Talking Picture of You (1929)
It All Depends on You (1926)
Sonny Boy (with Al Jolson) (1928)
Together (1928)
Varsity Drag (1927)
You're the Cream in My Coffee (1928)

JOHNNY BURKE
(1908-1964)

Music by Jimmy Van Heusen unless otherwise indicated.

Written for the stage:
1946 *Nelly Bly*
1953 *Carnival in Flanders*
1961 *Donnybrook* (music and lyrics)

Written for the screen (all released by Paramount except as noted):
1936 *Go West Young Man* (Arthur Johnston)
       Pennies from Heaven (Arthur Johnston - Columbia)
1938 *Doctor Rhythm*
1940 *Road to Singapore* (Victor Schertzinger)
1941 *Road to Zanzibar*
1942 *Road to Morocco*
1944 *Going My Way*
1945 *Road to Utopia*
1947 *Road to Rio*
1949 *A Connecticut Yankee in King Arthur's Court*
1950 *Riding High*
1952 *Road to Bali*

A selection of individual songs:
Aren't You Glad You're You (1945)
Going My Way (1944)
Here's That Rainy Day (featured in this folio - 1953)
Imagination (1940)
It Could Happen to You (1944)
Like Someone In Love (1944)
Misty (Erroll Garner) (1954)
Moonlight Becomes You (1942)
Oh, You Crazy Moon (1939)
Pennies from Heaven (Arthur Johnston) (1936)
Personality (1946)
Suddenly It's Spring (1944)
Sunday, Monday or Always (1943)
Swinging on a Star+ (1944)

IRVING CAESAR (Isidor Caesar)
(1895-1996)

Later in his career, Caesar wrote both words and music.

Written for the stage:
1925 *No, No Nanette* (co-lyricist with Otto Harbach; music by Vincent Youmans)
1929 *George White's Scandals* (co-lyricist with Cliff Friend; music by Friend and George White)
1931 *The Wonder Bar* (Robert Katscher)
1933 *Melody* (Sigmund Romberg)

Written for the screen:
1930 *No, No Nanette* (Vincent Youmans - Warner Brothers/First National)
1933 *The Kid from Spain* (one song with Harry Akst, Bert Kalmar and Harry Ruby - Goldwyn/UA)
1939 *At the Circus* (James V. Monaco - MGM)
1940 *No, No Nanette* (Vincent Youmans - RKO)
1950 *Tea for Two* (based on the show No, No Nanette) (Vincent Youmans - Warner Brothers)

A selection of individual songs:
Animal Crackers in My Soup (co-lyricist with Ted Koehler; music by Ray Henderson - 1935)
Crazy Rhythm (Joseph Meyer and Roger Wolfe Kahn; featured in this folio - 1928)
Just a Gigolo (Leonello Casucci - 1930)
I Want to be Happy (Vincent Youmans - 1924)
If I Forget You (1933)
Is It True What They Say About Dixie? (Sammy Lerner and Gerald Marks - 1936)
Sometimes I'm Happy (Vincent Youmans - 1926)
Swanee (George Gershwin - 1919)
Tea for Two (Vincent Youmans - 1924)

SAMMY CAHN (Samuel Cohen)
(1913-1993)

Cahn's earliest collaboration was with Saul Chaplin; his primary collaborators were Jule Styne and James Van Heusen.

Written for the stage:
1942 *High Button Shoes* (Styne)
1965 *Skyscraper* (Van Heusen)
1967 *Walking Happy* (Van Heusen)
1970 *Look to the Lilies* (Styne)
1974 *Words and Music* (a Broadway revue of Cahn's songwriting career; called *The Sammy Cahn Songbook* in London)

Written for the screen:
1940 *Ladies Must Live* (Chaplin - Warner Brothers/First National)
1943 *Thumbs Up* (Styne - Republic)
1944 *Step Lively* (Styne - RKO)
1947 *It Happened in Brooklyn* (Styne - MGM)
1948 *Romance on the High Seas* [UK title: It's Magic] (Styne - Warner. Brothers)
1949 *It's a Great Feeling* (Styne - Warner Brothers)
1952 *Because You're Mine* (Nicholas Brodszky - MGM)
       Peter Pan (Sammy Fain - Disney)
1956 *Meet Me in Las Vegas* (Brodszky - MGM)
1957 *The Joker Is Wild* (Van Heusen - Paramount)
1958 *The Long Hot Summer* (title song; Alex North - 20th Century-Fox)
1959 *A Hole in the Head* (Van Heusen - UA)
1960 *Let's Make Love* (Van Heusen - 20th Century-Fox)
1964 *Robin and the 7 Hoods* (Van Heusen - Warner Brothers)
1967 *Thoroughly Modern Millie* (Van Heusen - Universal)
1982 *Heidi's Song* (Burton Lane - Hanna-Barbera/Paramount)

A selection of individual songs:

All the Way+ (Van Heusen - 1957)
Be My Love (Brodszky - 1950)
Bei Mir Bist Du Schoen (Means That You're Grand) (1938)
    (Note: The song was originally written for the Yiddish theatre by
    Jacob Jacobs and Sholom Secunda. It was adapted as a pop song
    by Cahn and Chaplin.)
Call Me Irresponsible+ (Van Heusen; featured in this folio - 1963)
Day by Day (Paul Weston and Axel Stordahl - 1946)
Guess I'll Hang My Tears Out to Dry (Styne - 1945)
High Hopes+ (Van Heusen - 1959)
I'll Walk Alone (Styne - 1944)
I've Heard That Song Before (Styne - 1943)
It's Been a Long, Long Time (Styne - 1945)
Let It Snow! Let It Snow! Let It Snow! (Vaughn Monroe - 1946)
Love and Marriage (Van Heusen - 1955)
My Kind of Town (Chicago Is) (Van Heusen - 1964)
The Second Time Around (Van Heusen - 1960)
(Love Is) The Tender Trap (Van Heusen - 1955)
Thoroughly Modern Millie (Van Heusen - 1967)
Three Coins in the Fountain+ (Styne - 1954)
Time after Time (Styne - 1947)
Song from "Some Came Running" (To Love and Be Loved)
    (Van Heusen - 1958)

BETTY COMDEN and ADOLPH GREEN
(Both 1915-)

Comden and Green's primary collaborators were Leonard Bernstein, Jule Styne and Cy Coleman.

Written for the stage:
1944   *On the Town** (Bernstein)
1945   *Billion Dollar Baby** (Morton Gould)
1953   *Wonderful Town** (Bernstein)
1956   *Bells Are Ringing** (Styne)
1960   *Do Re Mi* (Styne)
1961   *Subways Are for Sleeping** (Styne)
1964   *Fade Out Fade In** (Styne)
1978   *On the Twentieth Century** (Coleman)
1982   *A Doll's Life** (Larry Grossman)
1991   *The Will Rogers Follies* (Coleman)

Written for the screen (MGM unless otherwise indicated):
1949   *The Barkleys of Broadway** [UK title: The Gay Barkleys] (Songs by
    Ira Gershwin and Harry Warren, one song by George and Ira Gershwin)
    *On the Town** (new score with Roger Edens, two songs with Bernstein
    retained)
    *Take Me Out to the Ball Game** (Edens)
1952   *Singin' in the Rain** (one song with Edens, score primarily by Arthur
    Freed and Nacio Herb Brown)
1953   *The Band Wagon** (score by Howard Dietz and Arthur Schwartz)
1955   *It's Always Fair Weather** (André Previn)
1958   *Auntie Mame** (songs by Jerome Lawrence, Robert E. Lee, Saul
    Schechtman - Warner Brothers)
1960   *Bells Are Ringing** (Styne)
1964   *What a Way to Go** (Styne - 20th Century-Fox)

A selection of individual songs:
Bells Are Ringing (1956)
The French Lesson (Roger Edens - 1947)
I Like Myself (André Previn - 1955)
Just in Time (Styne - 1956)
Lonely Town (Bernstein - 1944)
Long Before I Knew You (Styne - 1956)
Lucky to Be Me (Bernstein - 1944)
Make Someone Happy (Styne; featured in this folio - 1960)
Never Never Land (Styne - 1954)
New York, New York (Bernstein - 1944)
The Party's Over (Styne - 1956)

HAL DAVID
(1921-)

Music by Burt Bacharach unless otherwise indicated. Hal David is the brother of lyricist Mack David.

Written for the stage:
1968   *Promises, Promises* (1968)

Written for the screen:
1955   *The Rose Tattoo* (one song; Alex North - Paramount)
1956   *The Rainmaker* (title song; Alex North - Paramount)
1959   *That Kind of Woman* (song for exploitation only; not in film -
    Paramount)
1961   *The Man Who Shot Liberty Valance* (song for exploitation only; not in
    film - Paramount)
1962   *Hatari!* (one song; Henry Mancini - Paramount)
1963   *Wives and Lovers* (title song - Paramount)
1964   *Send Me No Flowers* (title song - Universal)
1965   *What's New, Pussycat?* (UA)
1966   *Promise Her Anything* (title song - Paramount)
1967   *Casino Royale* (Columbia)
1968   *Alfie* (title song - Paramount)
1969   *Butch Cassidy and the Sundance Kid* (20th Century-Fox)
1973   *Lost Horizon* (Columbia)
1975   *Return of the Pink Panther* (one song; Mancini - UA)

A selection of individual songs:
Alfie (featured in this folio - 1966)
Casino Royale (1967)
(They Long to Be) Close to You (1970)
Do You Know the Way to San Jose? (1968)
I'll Never Fall in Love Again (1968)
One Less Bell To Answer (1970)
Promises, Promises (1968)
Raindrops Keep Fallin' on My Head+ (1969)
This Guy's in Love with You (1968)
To All the Girls I've Loved Before (Albert Hammond 1975, 1984)
Trains and Boats and Planes (1965)
Walk On By (1961)
What the World Needs Now Is Love (1965)
What's New, Pussycat? (1965)
Wives and Lovers (1963)

HOWARD DIETZ
(1896-1983)

Music by Arthur Schwartz unless otherwise indicated.

Written for the stage:
1924   *Dear Sir* (Jerome Kern)
1926   *Oh, Kay!* (co-lyricist with Ira Gershwin on two songs; music
    by George Gershwin)
1929   *The Little Show* (also writer of most sketches; music by various
    composers)
1930   *Three's a Crowd* (also writer of some sketches; music by various
    composers)
1931   *The Band Wagon* (also writer of some sketches)
1932   *Flying Colors* (wrote all sketches; also director)
1934   *Revenge with Music**
1936   *The Show Is On* (numerous composers and lyricists)
1937   *Between the Devil**
1944   *Sadie Thompson* (lyricist and co-author of book with Rouben
    Mamoulian; music by Vernon Duke)
1948   *Inside U.S.A.*
1961   *The Gay Life*
1963   *Jennie*

Written for the screen:

1934 *The Girl from Missouri* (one song - MGM)
1936 *Under Your Spell* (20th Century-Fox)
1947 *Three Daring Daughters* (one song, Sammy Fain - MGM)
1953 *The Band Wagon* (MGM)

A selection of individual songs:

Alone Together (1932)
By Myself (featured in this folio - 1937)
Dancing in the Dark (1931)
I Guess I'll Have to Change My Plan (1929)
I See Your Face Before Me (1937)
Louisiana Hayride (1932)
Magic Moment (1961)
Moanin' Low (Ralph Rainger - 1929)
New Sun in the Sky (1931)
A Shine on Your Shoes (1932)
Something to Remember You By (1930)
That's Entertainment (1953)
You and the Night and the Music (1934)

FRED EBB
(1932-)

Music by John Kander.

Written for the stage:

1965 *Flora, the Red Menace*
1966 *Cabaret*
1968 *The Happy Time*
      Zorba
1971 *70, Girls, 70**
1974 *Liza*
1975 *Chicago**
1977 *The Act*
1981 *Woman of the Year*
1984 *The Rink*
1993 *Kiss of the Spider Woman*

Written for the screen:

1972 *Cabaret* (ABC/Allied Artists)
      Lucky Lady (20th Century-Fox)
1975 *Funny Lady* (Columbia)
1976 *A Matter of Time* (two songs - AIP)
1977 *New York, New York* (four songs - UA)

A selection of individual songs:

And All That Jazz (1975)
Believe (1971)
Cabaret (1966)
The Grass Is Always Greener (1981)
How Lucky Can You Get (1975)
If You Could See Her (1966)
Lucky Lady (1975)
Maybe This Time (1972)
My Coloring Book (1962)
(Theme from) New York, New York (Ebb collaborated on both words and
      music - 1977)
What Would You Do? (featured in this folio - 1966)
Willkommen (1966)

DOROTHY FIELDS
(1904-1974)

**Fields was the daughter of legendary producer Lew Fields, and
the sister of playwrights Joseph Fields and Herbert Fields.**

Written for the stage:

1928 *Blackbirds of 1928* (Jimmy McHugh)

1930 *International Revue* (Jimmy McHugh)
1939 *Stars in Your Eyes* (Arthur Schwartz)
1941 *Let's Face It* (book with Herbert Fields; score by Cole Porter)
1943 *Something for the Boys* (book with Herbert Fields; score by
      Cole Porter)
1944 *Mexican Hayride* (book with Herbert Fields; score by Cole Porter)
1946 *Annie Get Your Gun* (book with Herbert Fields; score by Irving Berlin)
1951 *A Tree Grows in Brooklyn* (Arthur Schwartz)
1966 *Sweet Charity* (Cy Coleman)
1973 *Seesaw* (Cy Coleman)

Written for the screen:

1930 *Love in the Rough* (Jimmy McHugh - MGM)
1935 *Every Night at Eight* (Jimmy McHugh - Paramount)
      I Dream Too Much (Jerome Kern - RKO)
1936 *Swing Time* (Jerome Kern - RKO)
1938 *The Joy of Living* (Jerome Kern - RKO)
1940 *One Night in the Tropics* (Jerome Kern - Universal)
1951 *Mr. Imperium* (Harold Arlen - MGM)
1953 *The Farmer Takes a Wife* (Harold Arlen - 20th Century-Fox)
1969 *Sweet Charity* (Cy Coleman - Universal)

A selection of individual songs:

(Hey) Big Spender (Cy Coleman - 1966)
Close as Pages in a Book (Sigmund Romberg - 1945)
Don't Blame Me (Jimmy McHugh - 1933)
Exactly Like You (Jimmy McHugh - 1930)
A Fine Romance (Jerome Kern; featured in this folio - 1936)
I Can't Give You Anything but Love (Jimmy McHugh - 1928)
I'm in the Mood for Love (Jimmy McHugh - 1935)
If My Friends Could See Me Now (Cy Coleman - 1965)
On the Sunny Side of the Street (Jimmy McHugh - 1930)
Pick Yourself Up (Jerome Kern - 1936)
Star in My Eyes (Fritz Kreisler - 1936)
The Way You Look Tonight+ (Jerome Kern - 1936)

IRA GERSHWIN (Israel Gershvin)
(1896-1983)

**Early in his career, Gershwin used the pseudonym Arthur
Francis, a combination of the names of his brother Arthur and
his sister Frances.**

Music by George Gershwin unless otherwise indicated.

Written for the stage:

1921 *Two Little Girls in Blue* (Vincent Youmans)
1924 *Lady Be Good!*
1925 *Tip-Toes*
1926 *Oh, Kay!*
1927 *Funny Face*
1928 *Show Girl* (on some songs, co-lyricist is Gus Kahn)
1930 *Girl Crazy*
      Strike Up the Band (revised from 1927 that closed out of town)
1931 *Of Thee I Sing* (winner of Pulitzer Prize)
1932 *Let' Em Eat Cake*
1935 *Porgy and Bess* (co-lyricist with DuBose Heyward)
1936 *Ziegfeld Follies* (Vernon Duke)
1941 *Lady in the Dark* (Kurt Weill)
1946 *Park Avenue* (Arthur Schwartz)
1983 *My One and Only*
1992 *Crazy for You*

Written for the screen:

1931 *Delicious* (Fox)
1932 *Girl Crazy* (RKO)
1937 *Shall We Dance* (RKO)
      A Damsel in Distress (RKO)
1943 *Girl Crazy* (MGM)

1944   *Cover Girl* (Jerome Kern - Columbia)
1945   *Where Do We Go from Here* (Kurt Weill 20th Century-Fox)
1947   *The Shocking Miss Pilgrim* (20th Century-Fox)
1949   *The Barkleys of Broadway* [UK title: *The Gay Barkleys*]
        (Harry Warren; one song by George Gershwin)
1951   *An American in Paris* (MGM)
1953   *Give a Girl a Break* (Burton Lane - MGM)
1954   *The Country Girl* (Harold Arlen - Paramount)
        A Star Is Born (new songs with Harold Arlen - Warner Brothers)
1964   *Kiss Me, Stupid* (UA)

A selection of individual songs:
Aren't You Kind of Glad We Did? (1947)
But Not for Me (1930)
Clap Yo' Hands (1926)
Do, Do, Do (1926)
Embraceable You (1930)
Fascinating Rhythm (1924)
A Foggy Day (1937)
Funny Face (1927)
How Long Has This Been Going On? (1928)
I Can't Get Started (Vernon Duke - 1936)
I Got Rhythm (1930)
I've Got A Crush on You (1930)
It Ain't Necessarily So (1935)
(The Saga of) Jenny (Kurt Weill - 1941)
Let's Call The Whole Thing Off (1937)
Long Ago and Far Away (Jerome Kern - 1944)
The Man I Love (1924)
The Man That Got Away (Harold Arlen; featured in this folio - 1954)
Nice Work If You Can Get It (1937)
'S Wonderful (1927)
Someone to Watch Over Me (1926)
They All Laughed (1937)
They Can't Take That Away from Me (1937)

MACK GORDON (Morris Gittler)
(1904-1959)

Gordon's primary collaborators were Harry Revel and Harry Warren.

Written for the stage:
1930   *Smile* (Vincent Youmans)
1931   *Fast and Furious* (two songs, Revel)
1932   *Smiling Faces* (Revel)

Written for the screen:
1933   *Sitting Pretty* (Revel - Paramount)
1934   *Belle of the Nineties* (Revel - Paramount)
        She Loves Me Not (Revel - Paramount)
        We're Not Dressing (Revel - Paramount)
1935   *Love in Bloom* (wrote words and music to four songs, one song with
        Revel; remainder of score primarily by Ray Noble - Paramount)
1936   *Poor Little Rich Girl* (Revel - 20th Century-Fox)
1937   *Wake Up and Live* (Revel - 20th Century-Fox)
        You Can't Have Everything (Revel - 20th Century-Fox)
1938   *Thanks for Everything* (Revel - 20th Century-Fox)
1939   *Rose of Washington Square* (one song, Revel - 20th Century-Fox)
1941   *Sun Valley Serenade* (Warren - 20th Century-Fox)
        That Night in Rio (Warren - 20th Century-Fox)
1942   *Iceland* (Warren - 20th Century-Fox)
        Orchestra Wives (Warren - 20th Century-Fox)
1943   *Sweet Rosie O'Grady* (Warren - 20th Century-Fox)
1944   *Sweet and Low-Down* (James V. Monaco - 20th Century-Fox)
1945   *The Dolly Sisters* (Monaco - 20th Century-Fox)
1947   *Mother Wore Tights* (Josef Myrow - 20th Century-Fox)
1948   *When My Baby Smiles at Me* (Myrow - 20th Century-Fox)

1950   *Summer Stock* (Warren; one song by Koehler and Arlen - MGM)
1953   *I Love Melvin* (Myrow - MGM)
1956   *Bundle of Joy* (Myrow - RKO)

A selection of individual songs:
At Last (Warren - 1942)
Chattanooga Choo Choo (Warren - 1941)
Did You Ever See a Dream Walking (Revel - 1933)
I Wish I Knew (Warren - 1945)
I've Got a Gal in Kalamazoo (Warren - 1942)
It's the Animal in Me (Revel - 1935)
The More I See You (Warren - 1945)
On the Boardwalk in Atlantic City (Myrow - 1946)
Paris in the Spring (Revel - 1935)
Serenade in Blue (Warren - 1942)
There Will Never Be Another You (Warren; featured in this folio - 1942)
Time on My Hands (co-lyricist with Harold Adamson, Vincent Youmans - 1930)
You Make Me Feel So Young (Josef Myrow - 1946)
You'll Never Know+ (Warren - 1943)

OSCAR HAMMERSTEIN II
(1895-1960)

Hammerstein's primary collaborators were Jerome Kern and Richard Rodgers.

Written for the stage:
1924   *RoseMarie** (co-author with Otto Harbach, music by Rudolf Friml and
        Herbert Stothart)
1925   *Sunny** (co-author with Otto Harbach, music by Jerome Kern)
1927   *Show Boat** (Jerome Kern)
1928   *The New Moon** (co-author with Frank Mandel and Laurence Schwab,
        music by Sigmund Romberg)
1929   *Sweet Adeline** (Kern)
1932   *Music in the Air** (Kern)
1934   *Three Sisters** (Kern)
1939   *Very Warm for May** (Kern)
1943   *Oklahoma!** (Rodgers)
1945   *Carousel** (Rodgers)
1947   *Allegro** (Rodgers)
1949   *South Pacific** (co-author with Josh Logan, music by Rodgers)
1951   *The King and I** (Rodgers)
1953   *Me and Juliet** (Rodgers)
1955   *Pipe Dream** (Rodgers)
1958   *Flower Drum Song** (co-author with Joseph Fields, music by Rodgers)
1959   *The Sound of Music** (co-author with Howard Lindsay and
        Russell Crouse, music by Rodgers)

Writtten for the screen:
1929   *The Desert Song* (Romberg - Warner Brothers)
        Show Boat (Kern - Universal)
        (Note: This was a silent film. There was a prologue added that featured
        some of the Hammerstein-Kern score.)
1930   *The New Moon* (Romberg - MGM)
        *Viennese Nights** (Romberg - Warner Brothers)
1934   *Music in the Air* (Kern - Fox)
1935   *Sweet Adeline* (Kern - Warner Brothers)
1936   *Show Boat** (Kern - Universal)
1937   *High, Wide and Handsome* (Kern - Paramount)
1940   *The New Moon* (Romberg - MGM)
1945   *State Fair** (Rodgers - 20th Century-Fox)
1951   *Show Boat* (Kern - MGM)
1955   *Oklahoma!* (Rodgers - Magna/20th Century-Fox)
1956   *Carousel* (Rodgers - 20th Century-Fox)
        The King and I (Rodgers - 20th Century-Fox)
1958   *South Pacific* (Rodgers - Magna/20th Century-Fox)
1961   *Flower Drum Song* (Rodgers - Universal)
1965   *The Sound of Music* (Rodgers - 20th Century-Fox)

A selection of individual songs:
All the Things You Are (Kern - 1939)
Bali Ha'i (Rodgers - 1949)
Climb Ev'ry Mountain (Rodgers - 1959)
Do-Re-Mi (Rodgers - 1959)
Don't Ever Leave Me (Kern - 1929)
The Folks Who Live on the Hill (Kern - 1937)
Getting to Know You (Rodgers - 1951)
Hello Young Lovers (Rodgers - 1951)
I Enjoy Being a Girl (Rodgers - 1958)
I Have Dreamed (Rodgers - 1951)
If I Loved You (Rodgers - 1945)
Indian Love Call (co-lyricist with Otto Harbach, music by Rudolf Friml - 1924)
It Might As Well Be Spring+ (Rodgers - 1945)
The Last Time I Saw Paris+ (Kern - 1941)
Lover, Come Back to Me (Romberg - 1928)
Make Believe (Kern - 1927)
My Favorite Things (Rodgers - 1959)
Oh, What a Beautiful Mornin' (Rodgers - 1943)
Ol' Man River (Kern - 1927)
People Will Say We're In Love (Rodgers - 1943)
Some Enchanted Evening (Rodgers - 1949)
The Song Is You (Kern - 1932)
Stouthearted Men (Romberg - 1928)
The Surrey with the Fringe on Top (Rodgers; featured in this folio - 1943)
This Nearly Was Mine (Rodgers - 1949)
Who? (co-lyricist with Otto Harbach, music by Kern - 1925)
Why Was I Born? (Kern - 1929)
You Are Love (Kern - 1927)
You'll Never Walk Alone (Rodgers - 1945)
Younger Than Springtime (Rodgers - 1949)

OTTO HARBACH (Otto Abels Hauerbach)
(1873-1963)

Harbach's frequent collaborators were Oscar Hammerstein II and Jerome Kern.

Written for the stage:
1908   *Three Twins* (Karl Hoschna)
1910   *Madame Sherry** (Karl Hoschna)
1912   *The Firefly** (Rudolf Friml)
1920   *Jimmie** (co-author with Frank Mandel; co-lyricist with Hammerstein, music by Herbert Stothart)
1922   *The Blue Kitten** (Rudolf Friml)
1923   *Kid Boots** (co-author with William Anthony McGuire; lyrics by Joseph McCarthy, music by Harry Tierney)
1924   *Rose-Marie** (co-author and co-lyricist with Hammerstein II, music by Herbert Stothart)
1925   *No, No Nanette** (co-author with Frank Mandel; lyrics by Irving Caesar, music by Vincent Youmans)
        *Sunny** (co-author and co-lyricist with Hammerstein, music by Kern)
1926   *The Desert Song** (co-author with Frank Mandel and Hammerstein; co-lyricist with Hammerstein, music by Sigmund Romberg)
1931   *The Cat and the Fiddle** (Kern)
1933   Roberta* (Kern)

Written for the screen:
1930   *Sunny* (co-lyricist with Hammerstein, music by Kern - Warner Brothers/First National)
1931   *Men of the Sky* (Kern - Warner Brothers/First National)
1933   *The Cat and the Fiddle* (Kern - MGM)
1935   *Roberta* (Kern - RKO)
1936   *RoseMarie* (co-lyricist with Hammerstein, music by Rudolf Friml - MGM)
1941   *Sunny* (co-lyricist with Hammerstein, music by Kern - Warner Brothers/First National)

1943   *The Desert Song* (co-lyricist with Hammerstein, music by Sigmund Romberg - Warner Brothers)
1952   *Lovely to Look At* [new version of *Roberta*] (Kern - MGM)
1953   *RoseMarie* (co-lyricist with Hammerstein, music by Rudolf Friml - MGM)

A selection of individual songs:
Bambalina (co-lyricist with Hammerstein, music by Vincent Youmans and Herbert Stothart - 1923)
Indian Love Call (co-lyricist with Hammerstein, music by Rudolf Friml - 1924)
A New Love is Old (Kern; featured in this folio - 1931)
The Night Was Made for Love (Kern - 1931)
Rose-Marie (co-lyricist with Hammerstein, music by Friml - 1924)
Smoke Gets in Your Eyes (Kern - 1933)
The Touch of Your Hand (Kern - 1933)
Who? (co-lyricist with Hammerstein, music by Kern - 1925)
Yesterdays (Kern - 1933)

E.Y. "YIP" HARBURG (Edgar Isidore Hochberg)
(1898-1981)

Harburg's primary collaborators were Harold Arlen and Burton Lane.

Written for the stage:
1929   *Earl Carroll's Sketchbook* (some sketches, five songs with Jay Gorney)
1932   *Walk a Little Faster* (co-lyricist with Charles Tobias, music by Vernon Duke)
1934   *Life Begins at 8:40* (co-lyricist with Ira Gershwin, music by Arlen)
1937   *Hooray for What?* (Arlen)
1940   *Hold On to Your Hats* (Lane)
1944   *Bloomer Girl* (also director; Arlen)
1947   *Finian's Rainbow** (co-author with Fred Saidy, music by Lane)
1951   *Flahooley** (co-author with Saidy, music by Sammy Fain)
1957   *Jamaica** (co-author with Saidy, music by Arlen)
1968   *Darling of the Day* (Jule Styne)

Written for the screen:
1933   *Moonlight and Pretzels* (Jay Gorney - Universal)
1936   *Gold Diggers of 1937* (Arlen - Warner Brothers/First National)
        The Singing Kid (Arlen - Warner Brothers/First National)
1939   *The Wizard of Oz* (Arlen - MGM)
1942   *Ship Ahoy* (Lane - MGM)
1944   *Meet the People* (Sammy Fain - MGM)
1962   *Gay Puree* (Arlen - UPA/Warner Brothers)
1968   *Finian's Rainbow** (co-screenwriter with Fred Saidy, music by Lane - Warner Brothers)

A selection of individual songs:
April in Paris (Vernon Duke - 1932)
Brother, Can You Spare a Dime? (Jay Gorney - 1932)
Can't Help Singing (Jerome Kern - 1944)
Ding-Dong! The Witch Is Dead (Arlen - 1939)
Happiness Is Just a Thing Called Joe (Arlen - 1943)
How Are Things in Glocca Morra? (Lane - 1946)
If This Isn't Love (Lane - 1947)
It's Only a Paper Moon (co-lyricist with Billy Rose, music by Arlen - 1933)
Last Night When We Were Young (Arlen - 1936)
Lydia the Tattooed Lady (Arlen - 1939)
Old Devil Moon (Lane - 1947)
Over the Rainbow+ (Arlen - 1939)
You're the Cure for What Ails Me (Arlen; featured in this folio - 1936)

SHELDON HARNICK
(1924-)

Music by Jerry Bock unless otherwise indicated.

Written for the stage:
1952 *New Faces of 1952* (one song, music and lyrics)
1958 *The Body Beautiful*
1959 *Fiorello!* (winner of Pulitzer Prize)
1960 *Tenderloin*
1963 *She Loves Me*
1964 *Fiddler on the Roof*
1966 *The Apple Tree*
1970 *The Rothschilds*
1976 *Rex* (Richard Rodgers)

Written for the screen:
1954 *New Faces* (one song, music and lyrics - 20th Century-Fox)
1971 *Fiddler on the Roof* (UA)
1984 *Blame It on Rio* (two songs, music by Cy Coleman - 20th Century-Fox)

A selection of individual songs:
Artificial Flowers (1960)
Boston Beguine (music and lyrics - 1952)
Dear Friend (1963)
Far From the Home I Love (1964)
Feelings (featured in this folio - 1966)
If I Were a Rich Man (1964)
Matchmaker, Matchmaker (1964)
The Shape of Things (music and lyrics - 1956)
She Loves Me (1963)
Sunrise, Sunset (1964)
To Life (L'Chaim) (1964)
When Did I Fall In Love (1959)

LORENZ HART
(1895-1943)

Except for a few early songs, Hart's sole collaborator was Richard Rodgers.

Written for the stage:
1925 *The Garrick Gaieties*
     Dearest Enemy
1926 *Betsy*
     The Girl Friend
1927 *A Connecticut Yankee*
1928 *Present Arms*
1929 *Spring is Here*
1930 *Simple Simon*
1931 *America's Sweetheart*
1935 *Jumbo*
1936 *On Your Toes** (co-author with Rodgers and George Abbott)
1937 *Babes in Arms** (co-author with Rodgers)
     I'd Rather Be Right
1938 *The Boys from Syracuse*
     I Married an Angel
1939 *Too Many Girls*
1940 *Higher and Higher*
     Pal Joey
1942 *By Jupiter** (co-author with Rodgers)

Written for the screen:
1930 *Heads Up!* (Paramount)
1931 *The Hot Heiress* (First National)
1932 *Love Me Tonight* (Paramount)
     The Phantom President (Paramount)

1933 *Hallelujah, I'm a Bum* [UK title: *Hallelujah, I'm a Tramp*] (UA)
1935 *Mississippi* (Paramount)
1939 *Babes in Arms* (MGM)
1940 *The Boys from Syracuse* (Universal)
     Too Many Girls (RKO)
1957 *Pal Joey* (Columbia)
1963 *Billy Rose's Jumbo* (MGM)

A selection of individual songs:
Bewitched, Bothered and Bewildered (1941)
Blue Moon (1934)
The Blue Room (1926)
Falling in Love with Love (1938)
Glad to Be Unhappy (1936)
Have You Met Miss Jones? (1937)
I Could Write a Book (1941)
I Didn't Know What Time It Was (1939)
I Wish I Were in Love Again (featured in this folio - 1937)
Isn't It Romantic? (1932)
It Never Entered My Mind (1940)
It's Easy to Remember (1935)
The Lady is a Tramp (1937)
Lover (1932)
Manhattan (1925)
My Funny Valentine (1937)
My Heart Stood Still (1927)
My Romance (1935)
Spring Is Here (1938)
There's a Small Hotel (1936)
This Can't Be Love (1938)
Where or When (1937)
With a Song in My Heart (1929)
You Took Advantage of Me (1928)

JERRY HERMAN (Gerald Herman)
(1933-)

Herman writes music and lyrics.

Written for the stage:
1961 *Milk and Honey*
1964 *Hello, Dolly!* (additional music and lyrics by Bob Merrill, Charles Strouse and Lee Adams)
1966 *Mame*
1969 *Dear World*
1974 *Mack and Mabel*
1979 *The Grand Tour*
1983 *La Cage aux Folles*

Written for the screen:
1969 *Hello, Dolly!* (20th Century-Fox)
1974 *Mame* (Warner Brothers)

A selection of individual songs:
Before the Parade Passes By (1964)
The Best of Times (1983)
Hello, Dolly! (1964)
I Am What I Am (1983)
I Won't Send Roses (featured in this folio - 1974)
If He Walked into My Life (1966)
It Only Takes a Moment (1964)
Mame (1966)
We Need a Little Christmas (1966)

TOM JONES
(1928-)

Music by Harvey Schmidt.

Written for the stage:
1960 *The Fantasticks*

1963 *110 in the Shade*
1966 *I Do! I Do!*
1969 *Celebration* (also director)
1970 *Colette*
1975 *Philemon*
1981 *Colette Collage*
1990 *The Bone Room*

A selection of individual songs:
The Honeymoon is Over (1967)
Is It Really Me? (1963)
Love Song (1969)
Much More (featured in this folio - 1960)
My Cup Runneth Over (1966)
Nevr Say No (1960)
Soon It's Gonna Rain (1960)
Try to Remember (1960)

GUS KAHN (Gustave Kahn)
(1886-1941)

Written for the stage:
1926 *Kitty's Kisses* (Con Conrad)
1928 *Whoopee!* (Walter Donaldson)
1929 *Show Girl* (co-lyricist with Ira Gershwin, music by George Gershwin)

Written for the screen:
1930 *Whoopee!* (Walter Donaldson - Goldwyn/UA)
1933 *Flying Down to Rio* (co-lyricist with Edward Eliscu, music by Vincent Youmans RKO)
1934 *Kid Millions* (Walter Donaldson - Goldwyn/UA)
The Merry Widow (co-lyricist with Lorenz Hart, music by Franz Lehar - MGM)
1935 *Thanks a Million* (Arthur Johnston - 20th Century Fox)
1936 *San Francisco* (Walter Jurmann and Bronislau Kaper - MGM)
1938 *The Girl of the Golden West* (Sigmund Romberg - MGM)
1939 *Honolulu* (music by Harry Warren - MGM)
1941 *Go West* (Bronislau Kaper - MGM)

A selection of individual songs:
Ain't We Got Fun? (co-writer with Richard Whiting and Raymond Egan - 1921)
Carioca (co-lyricist with Edward Eliscu, music by Vincent Youmans - 1933)
Carolina in the Morning (Walter Donaldson - 1922)
Day Dreaming (Jerome Kern - 1941)
Flying Down to Rio (co-lyricist with Edward Eliscu, music by Vincent Youmans - 1933)
It Had to Be You (Isham Jones - 1924)
Love Me or Leave Me (Walter Donaldson - 1928)
Makin' Whoopee! (Walter Donaldson; featured in this folio - 1928)
Memories (Egbert Van Alstyne - 1915)
My Buddy (Walter Donaldson - 1922)
The One I Love (Belongs to Somebody Else) (Isham Jones - 1924)
Pretty Baby (Egbert Van Alstyne and Tony Jackson - 1916)
San Francisco (Walter Jarmann and Bronislau Kaper - 1936)
Yes Sir, That's My Baby (Walter Donaldson - 1925)
You Stepped Out of a Dream (Nacio Herb Brown - 1940)

TED KOEHLER
(1894-1973)

Koehler's primary collaborator was Harold Arlen.

Written for the stage:
1930 *Earl Carroll's Vanities* (Arlen)
1934 *Just Say When* (Ray Henderson)

Written for the screen:

1933 *Let's Fall in Love* (Arlen - Columbia)
1935 *King of Burlesque* (Jimmy McHugh - 20th Century-Fox)
1936 *Dimples* (Jimmy McHugh - 20th Century-Fox)
1937 *Artist and Models* (Burton Lane - Paramount)
1938 *Start Cheering* (John Green - Columbia)
1944 *Up in Arms* (Arlen - Goldwyn/RKO)
1947 *My Wild Irish Rose* (M.K. Jerome - Warner Brothers)

A selection of individual songs (composer is Harold Arlen unless otherwise indicated):
Animal Crackers in My Soup (co-lyricist with Irving Caesar, music by Ray Henderson - 1935)
Between the Devil and the Deep Blue Sea (featured in this folio - 1931)
Dream a Little Dream of Me (Wilbur Schwandt and Fabian Andre - 1931)
Get Happy (1930)
I Love a Parade (1931)
I've Got the World on a String (1932)
Ill Wind (You're Blowin' Me No Good) (1934)
Let's Fall In Love (1933)
Now I Know (1944)
Stormy Weather (1933)
When the Sun Comes Out (1940)
Wrap Your Troubles in Dreams (co-lyricist with Billy Moll, music by Harry Barris 1931)

JOHN LATOUCHE
(1917-1956)

Written for the stage:
1937 *Pins and Needles* (sketches)
1940 *Cabin in the Sky* (Vernon Duke)
1946 *Beggar's Holiday** (Duke Ellington)
1954 *The Golden Apple** (Jerome Moross)
1956 *Candide* (only some lyrics; Latouche died in mid-production, music by Leonard Bernstein)

Written for the screen:
1954 *On the Waterfront* (title song for exploitation only, Leonard Bernstein - Columbia)

A selection of individual songs:
Ballad for Americans (cantata, music by Earl Robinson - 1939)
Brown Penny (Duke Ellington - 1946)
Cabin in the Sky (Vernon Duke - 1940)
Day Dream (Duke Ellington - 1941)
Honey in the Honeycomb (Vernon Duke - 1940)
Lazy Afternoon (Jerome Moross; featured in this folio - 1954)
Taking a Chance on Love (co-lyricist with Ted Fetter, music by Vernon Duke - 1940)

ALAN JAY LERNER
(1918-1986)

Music by Frederick Loewe unless otherwise indicated.

Written for the stage:

1945 *The Day Before Spring**
1947 *Brigadoon**
1948 *Love Life** (Kurt Weill)
1951 *Paint Your Wagon**
1956 *My Fair Lady**
1960 *Camelot**
1965 *On a Clear Day You Can See Forever** (Burton Lane)
1969 *Coco** (André Previn)
1973 *Gigi**
1976 *1600 Pennsylvania Avenue** (Leonard Bernstein)
1979 *Carmelina** (Burton Lane)
1983 *Dance a Little Closer** (also director; music by Charles Strouse)

Written for the screen:

1951 *Royal Wedding** [UK title: *Wedding Bells*] (Burton Lane - MGM)
     *An American in Paris** (songs by George and Ira Gershwin - MGM)
1954 *Brigadoon** (MGM)
1958 *Gigi** (MGM)
1964 *My Fair Lady** (Warner Brothers)
1969 *Paint Your Wagon** (Paramount)
1970 *On a Clear Day You Can See Forever** (Burton Lane - Paramount)
1974 *The Little Prince** (Paramount)

A selection of individual songs:

Almost Like Being in Love (1947)
Brigadoon (1947)
Camelot (1960)
Come Back to Me (Burton Lane - 1965)
Come to Me, Bend to Me (1947)
Get Me to the Church on Time (1956)
Gigi+ (1958)
The Heather on the Hill (1947)
Here I'll Stay (Kurt Weill - 1948)
I Could Have Danced All Night (1956)
I Remember It Well (1958)
I Talk to the Trees (1951)
I've Grown Accustomed to Her Face (featured in this folio - 1956)
If Ever I Would Leave You (1960)
On a Clear Day (Burton Lane - 1965)
The Rain in Spain (1956)
Thank Heaven for Little Girls (1958)
They Call the Wind Maria (1951)
Too Late Now (Burton Lane - 1951)
Wouldn't It Be Loverly? (1956)

FRANK LOESSER
(1910-1969)

From 1947 (and occasionally earlier), Loesser wrote both music and lyrics.

Written for the stage:

1948 *Where's Charley?*
1950 *Guys and Dolls*
1956 *The Most Happy Fella**
1960 *Greenwillow** (co-author with Lesser Samuels)
1961 *How to Succeed in Business without Really Trying*
     (winner of Pulitzer Prize)

Written for the screen:

1936 *The Man I Marry* (Irving Actman - Universal)
1939 *Destry Rides Again* (Frederick Hollander - Universal)
1940 *Buck Benny Rides Again* (Jimmy McHugh - Paramount)
1941 *Kiss the Boys Goodbye* (Victor Schertzinger - Paramount)
     Sis Hopkins (Jule Styne - Republic)
1942 *Sweater Girl* (Jule Styne - Paramount)
1943 *Thank Your Lucky Stars* (Arthur Schwartz - Warner Brothers)
1947 *Variety Girl* (RKO)
1949 *Neptune's Daughter* (MGM)
1950 Let's Dance (Paramount)
1952 *Hans Christian Andersen* (Goldwyn/RKO)
     Where's Charley? (Warner Brothers)
1955 *Guys and Dolls* (Goldwyn/MGM)
1967 *How to Succeed in Business without Really Trying* (UA)

A selection of individual songs:

Anywhere I Wonder (1952)
Baby, It's Cold Outside+ (1949)
Brotherhood of Man (1961)
Dolores (Louis Alter - 1941)
Guys and Dolls (1950)
Heart and Soul (Hoagy Carmichael - 1938)
How Sweet You Are (Arthur Schwartz - 1943)
I Believe in You (1961)
I Don't Want to Walk without You, Baby (Jule Styne - 1941)
I Wish I Didn't Love You So (1947)
I'll Know (1950)
I've Never Been in Love Before (1950)
If I Were a Bell (featured in this folio - 1950)
Inch Worm (1952)
Jingle, Jangle, Jingle (Joseph J. Lilley - 1942)
The Lady's in Love with You (Burton Lane - 1939)
Never Will I Marry (1960)
On a Slow Boat to China (1948)
Praise the Lord and Pass the Ammunition (1942)
Spring Will Be a Little Late This Year (1944)
Standing on the Corner (1956)
Wonderful Copenhagen (1952)

JOHNNY MERCER (John Herndon Mercer)
(1909-1976)

Written for the stage:

1940 *Walk with Music* (Hoagy Carmichael)
1946 *St. Louis Woman* (Harold Arlen)
1951 *Top Banana* (also composer)
1954 *House of Flowers* (Harold Arlen)
1956 *Li'l Abner* (Gene De Paul)
1959 *Saratoga* (Harold Arlen)

Written for the screen:

1937 *Ready, Willing and Able* (Richard Whiting - Warner Brothers)
1938 *Going Places* (Harry Warren - Warner Brothers/First National)
1941 *Blues in the Night* (Harold Arlen - Warner Brothers)
1942 *The Fleet's In* (Victor Schertzinger - Paramount)
     You Were Never Lovelier (Jerome Kern - Columbia)
1943 *The Sky's the Limit* (Harold Arlen - RKO)
1945 *The Harvey Girls* (Harry Warren - MGM)
1951 *The Belle of New York* (Harry Warren - MGM)
1953 *Top Banana* (also composer - UA)
1954 *Seven Brides for Seven Brothers* (Gene De Paul - MGM)
1955 *Daddy Long Legs* (also composer - 20th Century-Fox)
1959 *Li'l Abner* (Gene De Paul - Paramount)
1970 *Darling Lili* (Henry Mancini - Paramount)

A selection of individual songs:
And the Angels Sing (Ziggy Elman - 1939)
Arthur Murray Taught Me Dancing in a Hurry (Victor Schertzinger - 1942)
Autumn Leaves (Joseph Kosma - 1947)
Blues in the Night (Harold Arlen - 1941)
Come Rain or Come Shine (Harold Arlen - 1946)
Days of Wine and Roses+ (Henry Mancini - 1962)
Dearly Beloved (Jerome Kern - 1942)
Goody-Goody (Matty Malneck - 1936)
Hit the Road to Dreamland (Harold Arlen - 1942)
Hooray for Hollywood (Richard Whiting - 1938)
I'm an Old Cowhand (also composer - 1936)
I'm Old Fashioned (Jerome Kern - 1942)
Jeepers Creepers (Harry Warren - 1938)
Laura (David Raksin - 1944)
Moon River+ (Henry Mancini - 1961)
On the Atchison, Topeka and the Santa Fe+ (Harry Warren - 1945)
One for My Baby (And One More for the Road) (Harold Arlen;
      featured in this folio - 1943)
Skylark (Hoagy Carmichael - 1941)
Tangerine (Victor Schertzinger - 1942)
That Old Black Magic (Harold Arlen - 1943)
You Must Have Been a Beautiful Baby (Harry Warren - 1938)

MITCHELL PARISH
(1900-1993)

Written for the stage:
1987   *Stardust* (a revue of Parish's songs)

Written for the screen:
1934   *George White's Scandals of 1934* (two songs, Frank Perkins - Fox)
1952   *Ruby Gentry* (title song, Heinz Roemheld - 20th Century-Fox)

A selection of individual songs:
Blue Tango (Leroy Anderson - 1951)
Deep Purple (Peter DeRose - 1934)
Don't Be That Way (Edgar Sampson and Benny Goodman - 1938)
Moonlight Serenade (Glenn Miller - 1939)
Sleigh Ride (Leroy Anderson - 1950)
Sophisticated Lady (co-lyricist with Irving Mills; Duke Ellington - 1933)
Stairway to the Stars (Matty Malneck and Frank Signorelli - 1939)
Star Dust (Hoagy Carmichael; featured in this folio - 1929)
Stars Fell on Alabama (Frank Perkins - 1934)
Sweet Lorraine (Cliff Burwell - 1928)
Tzena, Tzena, Tzena (Issachar Miron and Julius Grossman - 1950)

COLE PORTER
(1891-1964)

Wrote music and lyrics.

Written for the stage:
1916   *See America First** (co-author and co-lyricist with
      Thomas Lawrason Riggs)
1929   *Fifty Million Frenchmen*
      Wake Up and Dream
1930   *The New Yorkers*
1932   *Gay Divorcee*
1934   *Anything Goes*
1935   *Jubilee*
1936   *Red, Hot and Blue!*
1939   *DuBarry Was a Lady*
1940   *Panama Hattie*
1944   *Mexican Hayride*
1948   *Kiss Me, Kate*

1950   *Out of This World*
1953   *Can-Can*
1955   *Silk Stockings*

Written for the screen:
1934   *The Gay Divorcee* (RKO)
1936   *Born to Dance* (MGM)
1937   *Rosalie* (MGM)
1940   *Broadway Melody of 1940* (MGM)
1941   *You'll Never Get Rich* (Columbia)
1943   *Let's Face It* (Paramount)
1946   *Night and Day* (Warner Brothers/First National)
1948   *The Pirate* (MGM)
1953   *Kiss Me, Kate* (MGM)
1956   *High Society* (MGM)
1957   *Silk Stockings* (MGM)
      Les Girls (MGM)
1960   *Can-Can* (20th Century-Fox)

A selection of individual songs:
All of You (1955)
Anything Goes (1934)
At Long Last Love (featured in this folio - 1938)
Be a Clown (1948)
Begin the Beguine (1935)
Blow, Gabriel, Blow (1934)
C'est Magnifique (1953)
Don't Fence Me In (1944)
Easy to Love (1936)
From This Moment On (1950)
I Concentrate on You (1940)
I Get a Kick Out of You (1934)
I Love Paris (1953)
I Love You (1944)
I've Got You Under My Skin (1936)
In the Still of the Night (1937)
Just One of Those Things (1935)
Let's Do It (Let's Fall in Love) (1928)
Love for Sale (1930)
Night and Day (1932)
So in Love (1948)
True Love (1956)
What Is This Thing Called Love? (1930)
You'd Be So Nice to Come Home To (1943)
You're the Top (1934)

TIM RICE (Timothy Miles Bindon)
(1944-)

Music by Andrew Lloyd Webber unless otherwise indicated.

Written for the stage:
1969   *Joseph and the Amazing Technicolor Dreamcoat*
1971   *Jesus Christ Superstar*
1976   *Evita*
1986   *Chess* (with Benny Andersson and Bjorn Ulvaeus)

Written for the screen:
1973   *Jesus Christ Superstar* (Universal)
1992   *Aladdin* (Alan Menken; Rice completed score begun
      by Howard Ashman - Disney)
1994   *The Lion King* (Elton John - Disney)
1996   *Evita* (Hollywood/Disney)

A selection of individual songs:
All Time High (John Barry - 1984)
Buenos Aires (1975)
Can You Feel the Love Tonight+ (Elton John - 1994)
Christmas Dream (1976)
Close Every Door (1969)
Don't Cry For Me Argentina (1976)
I Don't Know How to Love Him (1971)
I'd Be Surprisingly Good for You (featured in this folio - 1976)
Someone Else's Story (Benny Andersson and Bjorn Ulvaeus - 1988)
Superstar (1971)
A Whole New World+ (Alan Menken - 1992)

LEO ROBIN
(1900-1984)

Written for the stage:
1927 *Hit the Deck* (co-lyricist with Clifford Grey, music by Vincent Youmans)
1949 *Gentlemen Prefer Blondes* (Jule Styne)

Written for the screen:
1929 *Close Harmony* (Richard A. Whiting - Paramount)
1930 *Monte Carlo* (Whiting and W. Franke Harling - Paramount)
1932 *The Big Broadcast* (Ralph Rainger - Paramount)
       One Hour with You (Ralph Rainger - Paramount)
1933 *International House* (Rainger - Paramount)
1936 *The Big Broadcast of 1936* (Rainger and Whiting - Paramount)
1937 *Waikiki Wedding* (Rainger - Paramount)
1941 *Moon over Miami* (Rainger - 20th Century-Fox)
1943 *The Gang's All Here* (Harry Warren - 20th Century-Fox)
1946 *Centennial Summer* (principal lyricist, music by Jerome Kern - 20th Century-Fox)
1947 *Something in the Wind* (John Green - Universal)
1951 *Two Tickets to Broadway* (Jule Styne - RKO)
1953 *Gentlemen Prefer Blondes* (Jule Styne - 20th Century-Fox)
1955 *Hit the Deck* (co-lyricist with Clifford Grey, music by Vincent Youmans - MGM)
       My Sister Eileen (Jule Styne - Columbia)

A selection of individual songs:
Beyond the Blue Horizon (Richard A. Whiting and W. Franke Harling - 1930)
Blue Hawaii (Ralph Rainger - 1937)
Bye Bye Baby (Jule Styne - 1949)
Diamonds Are a Girl's Best Friend (Jule Styne - 1949)
Easy Living (Ralph Rainger - 1937)
A Gal in Calico (Arthur Schwartz - 1946)
Hallelujah! (co-lyricist with Clifford Grey, music by Vincent Youmans - 1927)
Hooray for Love (Harold Arlen - 1948)
If I Should Lose You (Ralph Rainger - 1935)
June in January (Ralph Rainger - 1934)
Louise (Richard A. Whiting - 1929)
Love in Bloom (Ralph Rainger - 1934)
Love Is Just Around the Corner (Lewis E. Gensler - 1935)
Please (Ralph Rainger - 1932)
Thanks for the Memory+ (Ralph Rainger; featured in this folio - 1938)
Up with the Lark (Jerome Kern - 1946)

STEPHEN SONDHEIM
(1930-)

Writes both music and lyrics, except as indicated.

Written for the stage:
1957 *West Side Story* (Leonard Bernstein)
1959 *Gypsy* (Jule Styne - 1959)
1962 *A Funny Thing Happened on the Way to the Forum*

1964 *Anyone Can Whistle*
1965 *Do I Hear a Waltz?* (Richard Rodgers)
1970 *Company*
1971 *Follies*
1973 *A Little Night Music*
1976 *Pacific Overtures*
1979 *Sweeney Todd, the Demon Barber of Fleet Street*
1980 *Marry Me a Little*
1981 *Merrily We Roll Along*
1984 *Sunday in the Park with George*
1987 *Into the Woods*
1991 *Assassins* (Off-Broadway and London)
1994 *Passion*

Written for the screen:
1961 *West Side Story* (Leonard Bernstein - Mirisch/UA)
1962 *Gypsy* (Jule Styne - Warner Brothers)
1966 *A Funny Thing Happened on the Way to the Forum* (UA)
1977 *A Little Night Music* (New World)
1990 *Dick Tracy* (Touchstone/Disney)

A selection of individual songs:
All I Need Is the Girl (Jule Styne - 1959)
Another Hundred People (1970)
Broadway Baby (1971)
Comedy Tonight (1962)
Everything's Coming Up Roses (Jule Styne - 1959)
Good Thing Going (1981)
I Feel Pretty (Leonard Bernstein - 1957)
The Ladies Who Lunch (featured in this folio - 1970)
Losing My Mind (1971)
Maria (Leonard Bernstein - 1957)
No One Is Alone (1987)
Putting It Together (1984)
Send in the Clowns (1973)
Somewhere (Leonard Bernstein - 1957)
Sooner or Later (I Always Get My Man)+ (1990)
Together Wherever We Go (Jule Styne - 1959)

P.G. WODEHOUSE (Pelham Grenville Wodehouse)
(1881-1975)

Music by Jerome Kern.

Written for the stage:
1917 *Leave It to Jane** (co-author with Guy Bolton)
       *Oh, Boy!** (co-author with Guy Bolton)
1918 *Oh, Lady! Lady!** (co-author with Guy Bolton)
1924 *Sitting Pretty*
1926 *Oh, Kay!** (co-author with Guy Bolton, score by George and Ira Gershwin)
1927 *Show Boat* (lyricist for song "Bill" originally written in 1918)
1928 *The Three Musketeers* (co-lyricist with Clifford Grey, music by Rudolf Friml)
1934 *Anything Goes** (co-author with Guy Bolton, score by Cole Porter)

Written for the screen:
1937 *A Damsel in Distress** (score by George and Ira Gershwin - RKO)

A selection of individual songs:
Bill (featured in this folio - 1918)
Cleopatterer (1917)
Have a Heart (1917)
The Land Where the Good Songs Go (1917)
Leave It to Jane (1917)
March of the Musketeers (co-lyricist with Clifford Grey - 1928)
Till the Clouds Roll By (1917)

At Long Last Love

from YOU NEVER KNOW

Words and Music by
COLE PORTER

I'm ___ so in love, ___ And though it gives me ___ joy in- tense, ___ I can't de-ci- pher, ___ If I'm a

Alfie
Theme from the Paramount Picture ALFIE

Words by HAL DAVID
Music by BURT BACHARACH

Very Slowly, Rubato

Be Our Guest
from Walt Disney's BEAUTY AND THE BEAST

Lyrics by HOWARD ASHMAN
Music by ALAN MENKEN

dining room proudly presents - your dinner! Be our guest! Be our guest! Put our ser - vice to the test. Tie your nap - kin 'round your neck, che - rie and we pro - vide the rest. Soup du jour! Hot hors d'oeuvres! Why, we

Bill
from SHOW BOAT

Lyrics by P.G. WODEHOUSE and OSCAR HAMMERSTEIN II
Music by JEROME KERN

JULIE:

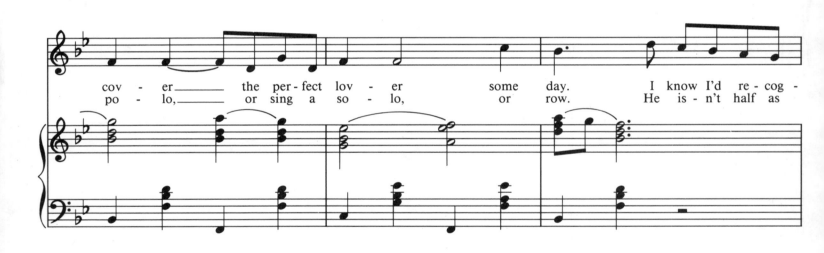

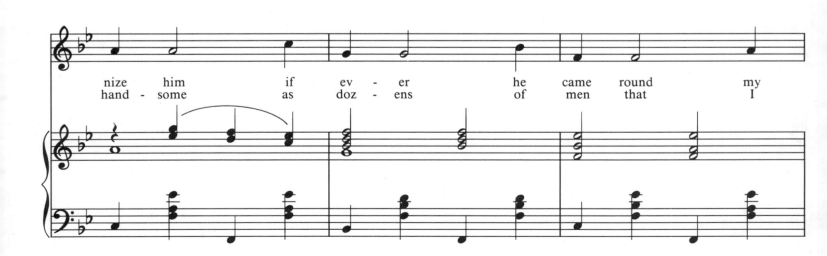

way.
I al - ways used to fan - cy then, He'd be

know.
He is - n't tall and straight and slim, And he

one of the god - like kind of men, With a gi - ant brain and a

dress - es far worse than Ted or Jim. Oh I can't ex - plain why he

no - ble head Like the he - roes bold In the books I've read. But a -

should be just the __ one, one bold man in the world for me. He's

long came Bill, who's not the type at all, You'd meet him on the street and nev - er

just my Bill, an or - di - na - ry guy, He has - n't got a thing that I can

pp

Between the Devil and the Deep Blue Sea

from RHYTHMANIA

Lyric by TED KOEHLER
Music by HAROLD ARLEN

By Myself

from BETWEEN THE DEVIL

Words by HOWARD DIETZ
Music by ARTHUR SCHWARTZ

46

Call Me Irresponsible

from the Paramount Picture PAPA'S DELICATE CONDITION

Words by SAMMY CAHN
Music by JAMES VAN HEUSEN

Crazy Rhythm

from THE COTTON CLUB

Words by IRVING CAESAR
Music by JOSEPH MEYER and ROGER WOLFE KAHN

Soon the high-brow, he has no brow, Ain't it a shame,

and you're to blame. What's the use of Pro-hi-bi-tion? You pro-duce the

same con-di-tion, Cra-zy Rhy-thm, I've gone cra-zy,

too.

too.

Feelings

from THE APPLE TREE

Words and Music by JERRY BOCK
and SHELDON HARNICK

Moderately

EVE:

[Repeat ad lib.]

Feel - ings are
I am the

tum-bling o-ver feel-ings, Feel-ings I do not un-der-stand. And I am
first to face this prob-lem, I am the first to have this dream. How can I

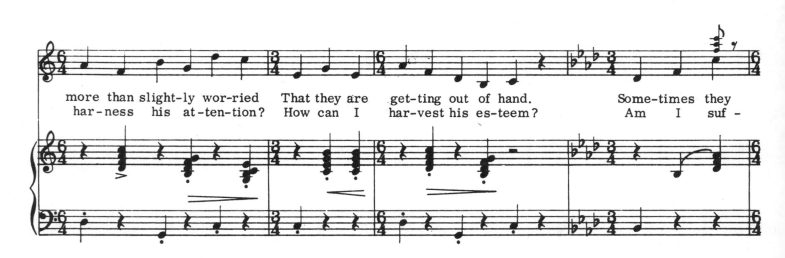

more than slight-ly wor-ried That they are get-ting out of hand. Some-times they
har-ness his at-ten-tion? How can I har-vest his es-teem? Am I suf-

A Fine Romance
from SWING TIME

Words by DOROTHY FIELDS
Music by JEROME KERN

Moderately (sung with sarcasm)

I don't need a moon, a nook, A tune - ful vi - o - lin. ___

Here's That Rainy Day

from CARNIVAL IN FLANDERS

Words by JOHNNY BURKE
Music by JIMMY VAN HEUSEN

May - be I should have saved those left o - ver

dreams; fun - ny, but here's that rain - y

day. Here's that rain - y day they

Button Up Your Overcoat

from FOLLOW THRU

Words and Music by B.G. DeSYLVA,
LEW BROWN and RAY HENDERSON

I Wish I Were in Love Again

from BABES IN ARMS

Words by LORENZ HART
Music by RICHARD RODGERS

This is a duet in the show.

love a-gain! No _ more care, No _ des - pair,

I'm _ all there now, _ But I'd rath - er be punch drunk! _ Be -

lieve me, sir, I much pre - fer the clas - sic bat - tle of a him and her, I

don't like qui - et and I wish I were in love a - gain!

I'd Be Surprisingly Good for You

from EVITA

Words by TIM RICE
Music by ANDREW LLOYD WEBBER

1. It seems cra-zy but you must be-lieve
   in like this

there's no-thing cal-cu-la-ted, no-thing planned
Twen-ty sec-onds af-ter say-ing hel-lo

Please for-give me if I
Tell-ing strang-ers I'm too

seem na-ive
good to miss

I would ne-ver want to force your hand: But
If I'm wrong I hope you'll tell me so: But you

please un-der-stand, I'd be good for you.
real-ly should know, I'd be good for you.

2. I don't al-ways rush

I Won't Send Roses

from MACK AND MABEL

Music and Lyric by
JERRY HERMAN

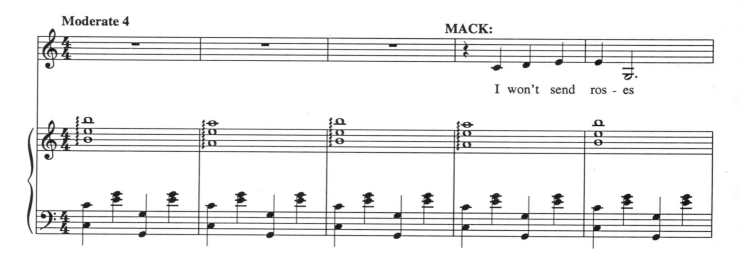

I won't send ros - es

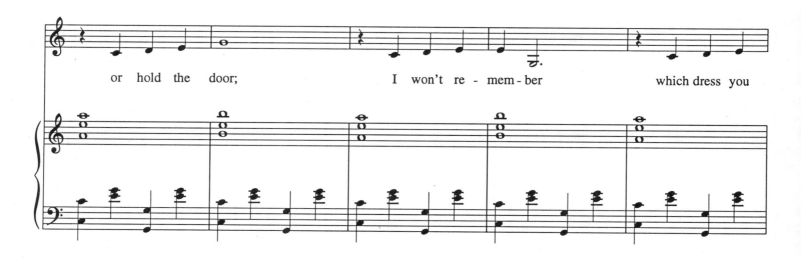

or hold the door; I won't re - mem - ber which dress you

wore. My heart is too much in con - trol, the lack of ro - mance in my soul

find things like guts and nerve, But not the kind things

that you de - serve. And so while there's a fight-ing chance just turn and

go. I won't send ros - es And ros - es suit

you so. _____

I've Grown Accustomed to Her Face
from MY FAIR LADY

Words by ALAN JAY LERNER
Music by FREDERICK LOEWE

HIGGINS: Marry Freddy! What an infantile idea! What a heartless, wicked, brainless thing to do. But she'll regret it. It's doomed before they even take the vow!

and lonely, repentant and contrite. Will I let her in or hurl her to

(Str. pizz.)

(±Bs.)

the wolves? Give her kindness, or the treatment she deserves?

(Vln. A
arco)

Will I take her back or throw the baggage

(Str. arco)
(W.W.)

Tranquillo

out? I'm a most forgiving man, The sort who

(Cl.)

(cued in Vln. A)

(Str.) (Hp.)

nev - er could, ev - er would Take a pos - i - tion and staunch-ly nev - er

(Str.) (+ W.W.)

Moderato con tenerezza *(tenderly)*

But I'm so used to hear her say "Good

morn-ing" ev-'ry day. Her joys, her woes, Her

highs, her lows, Are sec-ond na-ture to me now; —

Like breath-ing out and breath-ing in.

If I Were a Bell
from GUYS AND DOLLS

By FRANK LOESSER

Ask me how do I feel, lit - tle me with my qui - et up - bring - ing ____
Ask me how do I feel, Ask me now that we're fond - ly ca - ress - ing ____

Well, sir all I can say is, If I ____ were a gate I'd be swing - ing ____
_(Spoken) Pal, if I were a sal - ad I know ____ I'd be splashing my dress - ing ____

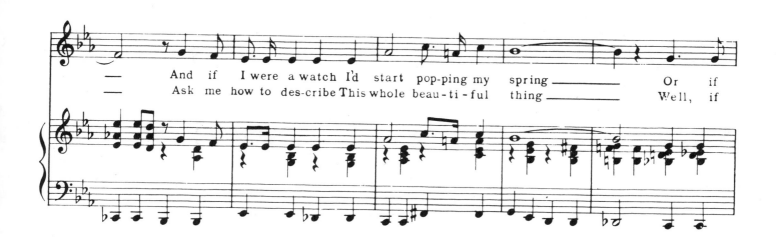

And if I were a watch I'd start pop - ping my spring ____ Or if
Ask me how to des-cribe This whole beau - ti - ful thing ____ Well, if

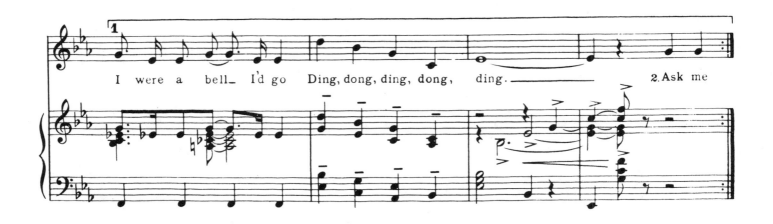

I were a bell_ I'd go Ding, dong, ding, dong, ding._____ 2. Ask me

I were a bell__ I'd go ding, dong, ding, dong,

ding._____

Make Someone Happy

from DO RE MI

Words by BETTY COMDEN and ADOLPH GREEN
Music by JULE STYNE

heart the heart you sing to.

One _____ smile that cheers you, One face that

lights when it nears you, One man you're ev - 'ry -

thing to. Fame, _____

poco rit. *a tempo*

found him, Build your world a - round him.

Make _____ some-one hap - py, Make just one _____

_____ some-one hap - py, And you _____ will be hap - py

too. Fame, _____

Lento

found him, Build your world a-round him.

Make _____ some-one hap - py, Make just one ____

____ some-one hap-py, And you _____ will be hap - py

Più mosso (in 4)   Marcato

too. _____

mf   *f*   *ff*

The Ladies Who Lunch

from COMPANY

Music and Lyrics by
STEPHEN SONDHEIM

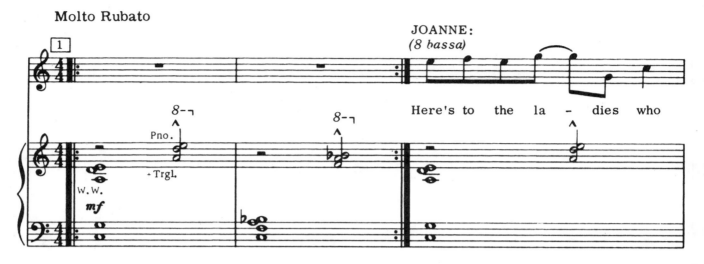

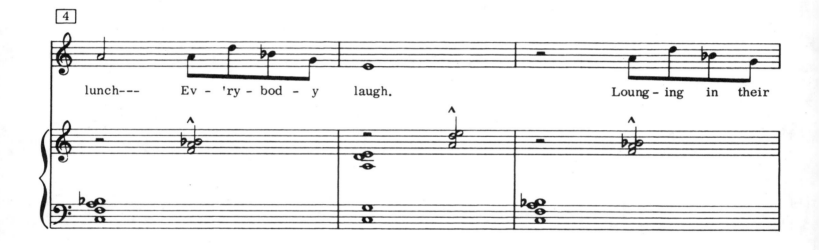

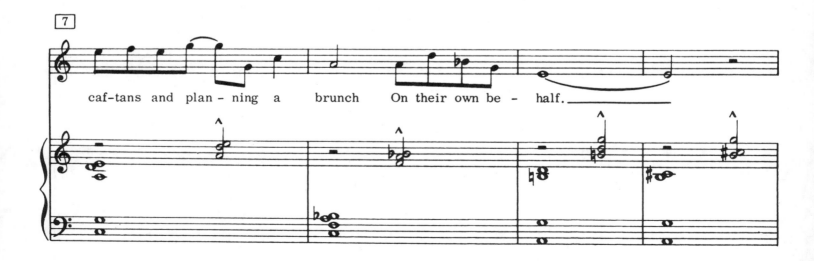

Rush-ing to their class-es in op - ti-cal art,___ Wish-ing it would

pass. An-oth-er long, ex-haust-ing day,___

Str., Hns., Fl.

An-oth-er thou-sand dol-lars.___ A mat-i-nee: A

(+Hns., Trbs. sust.)
mp

Pin-ter play,___ Per-haps a piece of Mah - ler's.___ I'll drink to

[Scream]

not to move,___ An-oth-er vod-ka sting - er. Aaah___

___ I'll drink to that. So

here's to the girls___ on the go,___ Ev-'ry-bod-y tries.

Look in-to their eyes and you'll see___ what they know:___ Ev-'ry-bod-y

+Bar. Sax.

+Str. sust.

+Bar. Sax.

91

dies._____ A toast to that in-vin-ci-ble bunch,___

+Hns., Trbs., Saxs.

(+Hns., Trbs. sust.)

94

+Tpts.

___ The di-no-saurs sur-viv-ing the crunch,___ Let's

[2 times]

97

hear it for the la-dies who lunch:___ Ev-'ry-bod-y rise!_____

+Saxs.

Tpts.

f Hns., Trbs., Saxs.

+Timp._____

101 [3 times]

Rise! Rise! Rise!_____

Tpts.

[As she drops hands]

cresc.

+Timp._____

Lazy Afternoon

from THE GOLDEN APPLE

Words by JOHN LATOUCHE
Music by JEROME MOROSS

It's a la - zy af - ter - noon and the bee - tle bugs are zoom - in' and the tu - lip trees are bloom - in' and there's not an - oth - er hu - man in view but us

Makin' Whoopee!

from WHOOPEE!

Lyrics by GUS KAHN
Music by WALTER DONALDSON

The Man That Got Away

from the Motion Picture A STAR IS BORN

Lyric by IRA GERSHWIN
Music by HAROLD ARLEN

Much More
from THE FANTASTICKS

Words by TOM JONES
Music by HARVEY SCHMIDT

LUISA: **Con moto** ♩ = 120

I'd like to swim in a clear blue stream Where the wa - ter is i - cy

p legato

cold; Then go to town in a gold - en gown And

have my for - tune told. Just

once! Just once! Just once be - fore I'm

mf

*small notes are optional throughout.

old! I'd like to be not e - vil, But a

lit - tle world - ly wise. To be the kind of

girl de - signed To be kissed up - on the eyes. I'd

(Same tempo - non accel.)

like to dance till two o' - clock Or some-times dance till

pp *poco a poco cresc.*

(no pedal)

A New Love Is Old

from THE CAT AND THE FIDDLE

Words by OTTO HARBACH
Music by JEROME KERN

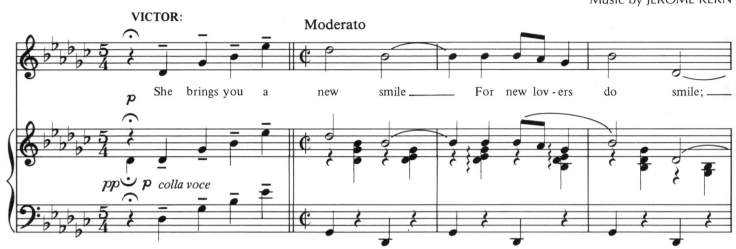

Take what she of-fers and be gay;

Love hates a man who runs a - way.

Hot, ea - ger lips can smoth-er

Thoughts, that re - call an-oth - er day._____ She brings you a

new smile,_____ For new lov - ers do smile._____

One for My Baby

(And One More for the Road)

from the Motion Picture THE SKY'S THE LIMIT

Lyric by JOHNNY MERCER
Music by HAROLD ARLEN

Puttin' On the Ritz
from the Motion Picture PUTTIN' ON THE RITZ

Words and Music by
IRVING BERLIN

Star Dust

Words by MITCHELL PARISH
Music by HOAGY CARMICHAEL

won - der why I spend the lone - ly night

dream-ing of a song? The mel - o - dy haunts my rev - er - ie,

and I am once a - gain with you, _____ when our

love was new, and each kiss an in - spi - ra - tion. _____

The Surrey with the Fringe on Top

from OKLAHOMA!

Lyrics by OSCAR HAMMERSTEIN II
Music by RICHARD RODGERS

Tempo giusto

Two bright side lights, wink-in' and blink-in' Ain't no fin - er

rig, I'm a-think-in'! You c'n keep yer rig if you're think-in' 'at I'd

keer to swop fer that shin - y lit - tle sur - rey with the

fringe on the top!

Brightly

Tempo giusto

All the world -'ll fly in a flur - ry When I take you out in the sur - rey When I take you out in the sur - rey with the fringe on top! When we hit that road, hell fer leath - er, Cats and dogs -'ll dance in the heath - er

156

Con sentimento (*slowly*)

CURLY: *sings*

I can see the stars git-tin' blur-ry When we ride back home in the sur-rey, Rid-in' slow-ly home in the sur-rey with the fringe on top. I can feel the day git-tin' old-er, Feel a sleep-y-head near my shoul-der,

Nod-din', droop-in' close to my shoul-der till it falls, ker-plop! The sun is swim-min' on the rim of a hill, The moon is tak-in' a head-er, And jist as I'm think-in' all the earth is still, A lark-'ll wake up in the med-der.

Hush! You bird, my ba-by's a-sleep-in'— May-be got a dream worth a-keep-in'— Whoa! you team, and jist keep a-creep-in' at a slow clip clop. Don't you hur-ry with the sur-rey with the fringe on the top.

Thanks for the Memory

from the Paramount Picture THE BIG BROADCAST OF 1938

Words and Music by LEO ROBIN
and RALPH RAINGER

What Would You Do?

from the Musical CABARET

Words by FRED EBB
Music by JOHN KANDER

cue: FRAULEIN SCHNEIDER: It's easy for you to say "fight"!

day is done. Grown wise like me, Who is-n't at war with

an - y - one, Not an - y more!

storm in the wind, What would you do? Sup-

pose you're one fright-ened voice   Be-ing told what the choice   must

be,   Go on, tell me,   I will

lis - ten.   What would you do   if

you were me?

You're the Cure for What Ails Me

from the Motion Picture THE SINGING KID

Lyric by E.Y. HARBURG
Music by HAROLD ARLEN

PIANO

I was born a del-i-cate child, Watched the oth-er kids run wild, While they played with guns and ropes, My on-ly toys were steth-o-scopes;

poco rit.

Vamp

(Rhythmically)

*Symbols are for Ukulele, Banjo and Guitar

There Will Never Be Another You

from the Motion Picture ICELAND

Lyric by MACK GORDON
Music by HARRY WARREN